TYRA
BANKS

TYRA BANKS

Pam Levin

CHELSEA HOUSE PUBLISHERS
Philadelphia

Cover photo: © Dennis Van Tine/London Features International

Chelsea House Publishers

Editor in Chief	Stephen Reginald
Production Manager	Pamela Loos
Director of Photography	Judy L. Hasday
Art Director	Sara Davis
Managing Editor	James D. Gallagher
Senior Production Editor	LeeAnne Gelletly

Staff for TYRA BANKS

Prepared by	21st Century Publishing and Communications, New York
Associate Art Director	Takeshi Takahashi
Cover Designer	Brian Wible

The Chelsea House World Wide Website is
http://www.chelseahouse.com

First Printing

1 3 5 7 9 8 6 4 2

Library of Congress Cataloging-in-Publication Data

Applied for
ISBN 0-7910-5195-1 (hc)
        0-7910-5196-X (pb)

Frontis:
Relaxed and smiling, Tyra Banks reflects what has been described as her natural beauty both inside as well as outside.

CONTENTS

BLACK AMERICANS OF ACHIEVEMENT

HENRY AARON
baseball great

KAREEM ABDUL-JABBAR
basketball great

MUHAMMAD ALI
heavyweight champion

RICHARD ALLEN
*religious leader and
social activist*

MAYA ANGELOU
author

LOUIS ARMSTRONG
musician

ARTHUR ASHE
tennis great

JOSEPHINE BAKER
entertainer

JAMES BALDWIN
author

TYRA BANKS
model

BENJAMIN BANNEKER
scientist and mathematician

AMIRI BARAKA
poet and playwright

COUNT BASIE
bandleader and composer

ROMARE BEARDEN
artist

JAMES BECKWOURTH
frontiersman

MARY MCLEOD BETHUNE
educator

GEORGE WASHINGTON
CARVER
botanist

CHARLES CHESNUTT
author

JOHNNIE COCHRAN
lawyer

BILL COSBY
entertainer

PAUL CUFFE
merchant and abolitionist

MILES DAVIS
musician

FATHER DIVINE
religious leader

FREDERICK DOUGLASS
abolitionist editor

CHARLES DREW
physician

W. E. B. DU BOIS
scholar and activist

PAUL LAURENCE DUNBAR
poet

DUKE ELLINGTON
bandleader and composer

RALPH ELLISON
author

JULIUS ERVING
basketball great

LOUIS FARRAKHAN
political activist

ELLA FITZGERALD
singer

MORGAN FREEMAN
actor

MARCUS GARVEY
black nationalist leader

JOSH GIBSON
baseball great

WHOOPI GOLDBERG
entertainer

CUBA GOODING JR.
actor

ALEX HALEY
author

PRINCE HALL
social reformer

JIMI HENDRIX
musician

MATTHEW HENSON
explorer

GREGORY HINES
performer

BILLIE HOLIDAY
singer

LENA HORNE
entertainer

WHITNEY HOUSTON
singer and actress

LANGSTON HUGHES
poet

ZORA NEALE HURSTON
author

JANET JACKSON
singer

JESSE JACKSON
civil-rights leader and politician

MICHAEL JACKSON
entertainer

SAMUEL L. JACKSON
actor

T. D. JAKES
religious leader

JACK JOHNSON
heavyweight champion

MAGIC JOHNSON
basketball great

SCOTT JOPLIN
composer

BARBARA JORDAN
politician

MICHAEL JORDAN
basketball great

CORETTA SCOTT KING
civil-rights leader

MARTIN LUTHER KING JR.
civil-rights leader

LEWIS LATIMER
scientist

SPIKE LEE
filmmaker

CARL LEWIS
champion athlete

JOE LOUIS
heavyweight champion

RONALD MCNAIR
astronaut

MALCOLM X
militant black leader

BOB MARLEY
musician

THURGOOD MARSHALL
Supreme Court justice

TONI MORRISON
author

ELIJAH MUHAMMAD
religious leader

EDDIE MURPHY
entertainer

JESSE OWENS
champion athlete

SATCHEL PAIGE
baseball great

CHARLIE PARKER
musician

ROSA PARKS
civil-rights leader

COLIN POWELL
military leader

PAUL ROBESON
singer and actor

JACKIE ROBINSON
baseball great

CHRIS ROCK
comedian/actor

DIANA ROSS
entertainer

WILL SMITH
actor

CLARENCE THOMAS
Supreme Court justice

SOJOURNER TRUTH
antislavery activist

HARRIET TUBMAN
antislavery activist

NAT TURNER
slave revolt leader

TINA TURNER
entertainer

DENMARK VESEY
slave revolt leader

ALICE WALKER
author

MADAM C. J. WALKER
entrepreneur

BOOKER T. WASHINGTON
educator

DENZEL WASHINGTON
actor

J. C. WATTS
politician

VANESSA WILLIAMS
singer and actress

OPRAH WINFREY
entertainer

TIGER WOODS
golf star

RICHARD WRIGHT
author

ON
ACHIEVEMENT

———— ❦ ————

Coretta Scott King

BEFORE YOU BEGIN this book, I hope you will ask yourself what the word *excellence* means to you. I think it's a question we should all ask, and keep asking as we grow older and change. Because the truest answer to it should never change. When you think of excellence, perhaps you think of success at work; or of becoming wealthy; or meeting the right person, getting married, and having a good family life.

Those goals are worth striving for, but there is a better way to look at excellence. As Martin Luther King Jr. said in one of his last sermons, "I want you to be first in love. I want you to be first in moral excellence. I want you to be first in generosity. If you want to be important, wonderful. If you want to be great, wonderful. But recognize that he who is greatest among you shall be your servant."

My husband knew that the true meaning of achievement is service. When I met him, in 1952, he was already ordained as a Baptist minister and was working toward a doctoral degree at Boston University. I was studying at the New England Conservatory and dreamed of accomplishments in music. We married a year later, and after I graduated the following year we moved to Montgomery, Alabama. We didn't know it then, but our notions of achievement were about to undergo a dramatic change.

You may have read or heard about what happened next. What began with the boycott of a local bus line grew into a national crusade, and by the time he was assassinated in 1968 my husband had fashioned a black movement powerful enough to shatter forever the practice of racial segregation. What you may not have read about is where he learned to resist injustice without compromising his religious beliefs.

He adopted a strategy of nonviolence from a man of a different race, who lived in a different country and even practiced a different religion. The man was Mahatma Gandhi, the great leader of India, who devoted his life to serving humanity in the spirit of love and nonviolence. It was in these principles that Martin discovered his method for social reform. More than anything else, those two principles were the key to his achievements.

These books are about African Americans who served society through the excellence of their achievements. They form part of the rich history of black men and women in America—a history of stunning accomplishments in every field of human endeavor, from literature and art to science, industry, education, diplomacy, athletics, jurisprudence, even polar exploration.

Not all of the people in this history had the same ideals, but I think you will find that all of them had something in common. Like Martin Luther King Jr., they all decided to become "drum majors" and serve humanity. In that principle—whether it was expressed in books, inventions, or song—they found a goal and a guide outside themselves that showed them a way to serve others instead of living only for themselves.

Reading the stories of these courageous men and women not only helps us discover the principles that we will use to guide our own lives; it also teaches us about our black heritage and about America itself. It is crucial for us to know the heroes and heroines of our history and to realize that the price we paid in our struggle for equality in America was dear. But we must also understand that we have gotten as far as we have partly because America's democratic system and ideals made it possible.

We are still struggling with racism and prejudice. But the great men and women in this series are a tribute to the spirit of the country in which they have flourished. And that makes their stories special and worth knowing.

1

MANY BEAUTIFUL FACES:
SUCCESS ON HER OWN TERMS

— ❧ —

T ALL AND POISED in a pale lavender dress, supermodel Tyra Banks stood behind the podium, addressing an audience of young women. Along with Secretary of Health and Human Services Donna Shalala and Tipper Gore, wife of Vice President Al Gore, Tyra was a featured speaker at the Volunteerism Awards luncheon held on March 31, 1998, in Washington, D.C.

The event, sponsored by *Seventeen* magazine and Cover Girl cosmetics, honored the winners of the 1998 Volunteerism Awards. In response to President Clinton's call for volunteerism and public service, the magazine and the cosmetics company had joined in a partnership to honor young women who had done "extraordinary things that help ordinary people." Cover Girl and *Seventeen* exert a strong influence on teenagers, and the companies were anxious to use their prestige to make young women aware of the importance of community service. *Seventeen* announced the award in its August 1997 issue and followed up with ads calling upon young women to enter the contest. Cover Girl included a feature on volunteerism in its educational publication, *Seventeen at School*, which is read by students around the nation. The broadcast media and cyberspace were also used. Cover Girl sponsored radio ads nationwide and included entry

At a news conference following the 1998 Volunteerism Awards ceremony, Tyra shares the spotlight with Senator John Warner and one of the young award winners, Amity Weiss. Tyra tirelessly encourages young people to overcome life's challenges and find success on their own terms, as she has.

Tyra does not just lend her name to a project, as do many celebrities. She is an active participant in programs she sponsors, preferring, as she says, "one-on-one contact" with others. Here she shares a story with kids at The Center for Children + Families.

information on its website, and *Seventeen* informed teens on America Online.

Cover Girl and *Seventeen* are longtime clients of supermodel Tyra Banks, a tireless advocate of community service, and they asked her to attend the awards ceremony to promote volunteerism. Tyra readily accepted. At age 24, Tyra Banks's beautiful image had earned her millions of dollars. Her face had graced the covers of hundreds of magazines and had appeared in countless others. She had made television commercials and had been featured on television shows and in videos and films. And she had just written a book, *Tyra's Beauty, Inside and Out*. She had accomplished all of this in only seven years. However, she was an appropriate speaker, as volunteerism is a top priority in her life. In keeping with what she has called her passion to help children, she is a spokesperson for The Center for Children + Families in New York City, an organization devoted to helping abused and neglected kids. Through the center, she has promoted a line of greeting cards. Called Cards from the Heart by Tyra's Kidsuccess Kids, the cards are created by children aged eight and nine in an after-school arts and reading program, which is part of a literacy project. In addition to backing worthy projects, Tyra spends a great deal of time with the children at the center, reading and painting together. She has acknowledged that she spends so much time with the children that they are not the least bit impressed with her celebrity status.

Another project dear to Tyra's heart was the Kidshare toy drive she sponsored for the center. The idea was to have children experience the joy of giving a gift to someone else. Since the kids could not afford to buy gifts, Tyra campaigned for corporations and the public to donate gifts that the children could give to one another. Tyra said of this experience, "I wish I could describe how seeing all those happy, excited faces made me feel, but I don't think words would do it justice." For her commitment and dedication to children, the Starlight Children's Foundation of California honored Tyra with its Friendship Award in 1997.

Tyra has also established a Tyra Banks Scholarship for young African-American girls to attend her own high school, Immaculate Heart, in Los Angeles. She explains how her experiences at the school led her to establish the scholarship: "I was privileged to be able to attend such a fine school, led by women who were such good role models. . . . I established [the scholarship] there so that other young women less fortunate than I can have the same opportunity." As Tyra has said in encouraging young women to help others, "Well it's just really beautiful and wonderful, you know, to really help people, but it also makes you feel good about yourself, and I really believe in strong self-esteem, especially with young women."

The teens at the awards luncheon listened intently as Tyra said, "It's important to love what you see in the mirror, but it's even more important how you feel about what you see in the mirror." The young winners were examples of just what Tyra meant when she went on to tell them how doing things for others could bring self-respect and confidence. They were winners in a contest in which personal efforts to improve the lives of others and accomplishments in community service were more important than personal appearance. What one did mattered more than how one looked. As the sponsors announced, winners were chosen "because of their extraordinary commitment to volunteerism and public service, their demonstrated leadership and responsibility, and the impact their efforts have had on others."

In recognizing the young volunteers' achievements, the sponsors awarded more than $100,000 in scholarships and U.S. savings bonds. Ranging in age from 14 to 21 years old, the young women were judged in three age groups: 13 to 15, 16 to 18, and 19 to 21, with two winners in each category. The three top winners each received a $20,000 scholarship; each of the three second-place winners was awarded a $10,000 scholarship. In addition to attending the awards ceremony, the top six young women were featured in *Seventeen* magazine. There were also 24 runners-up, and they each received a $1,000 savings bond and honorable mention in *Seventeen*.

The young nominees were judged on several factors: their commitment to volunteering for public service, their level of responsibility and leadership qualities, the uniqueness of their efforts, the impact made on their area of service, and the success of their efforts. The winners' accomplishments ranged from founding a group to help the homeless to lobbying to keep a public library open.

At age 13, Amber Coffman of Glen Burnie, Maryland, founded Happy Helpers for the Homeless, which provides food and other necessities as well as resource information to people living on the streets in her hometown and in Baltimore. At age 16, when she won the award, Amber was preparing 600 lunches every week for the needy and was involved in developing a guide for others who wanted to begin similar programs. Upon finding that her public library was going to close, La-Kee-A Lowry of Brooklyn, New York, started a petition and collected 1,500 signatures. She organized classmates to write letters to the White House and to Congress. Through her efforts, the library remained open. Twenty-one at the time of the award, La-Kee-A was working with children to encourage reading.

Other winners included Amity Weiss of Ithaca, New York, who organized a children's march and fundraisers for a troubled town in Bosnia, which eventually became Ithaca's sister city. Lindsay Neil

Appearing at the Volunteerism Awards ceremony gave Tyra the opportunity to promote a cause dear to her heart— encouraging young people to become active in public service. Here she is surrounded by the award winners. From left are Lindsay Neil, Amber Coffman, Amity Weiss, Gillian Kilberg, Christin Brown, and La-Kee-A Lowry.

of Greeley, Colorado, raised a million pennies to build a high school for a poor village in Nicaragua and then actually helped construct the building. Cristin Brown of Wisner, Nebraska, organized a farm-safety program and conducted workshops in local schools. Gillian Kilberg of McLean, Virginia, used an inheritance to found a special summer camp for needy and abused children.

As Tyra Banks spoke at the awards ceremony, she was proud to be a role model, a person whom others could emulate. She was using her famous image to support and encourage young women, who often watched her carefully and wanted to be like her. She could spur them to take control of their lives, stand up for their beliefs, and give of themselves. She wanted all young women, regardless of their looks or situations, to have the confidence and self-esteem to be good enough to overcome the self-doubts, peer pressures, and body-image discomforts that teens commonly encounter.

Tyra's own image did not always radiate confidence. As she was growing up, she experienced name calling, parental divorce, and insecurities that, she claims, eventually strengthened her. From a skinny, awkward, extremely tall 11-year-old, she transformed herself into the woman who possesses the flawless, golden-brown skin, exotic eyes, and slim, long-legged figure for which she has become famous.

In fewer than 10 years, Tyra has become extraordinarily well paid to present her unique beauty in print and on film worldwide. *People* magazine has named her one of the 50 Most Beautiful People in the world—twice. She is only the third African-American model to sign an exclusive contract with a major cosmetics company and the first African-American woman to appear on the cover of *Sports Illustrated Swimsuit Issue*. Tyra is also the first black model to grace the cover of the Victoria's Secret catalog and *GQ* magazine. Major advertisers seek her out to model products both in print and on television. As a young black woman, Tyra has gained respect for creating a black presence in the mainstream fashion and advertising world. As an entrepreneur, she heads her own corporation, Bankable, Inc. Tyra Banks is very much in control of her own destiny.

By 1997, Tyra had created an extraordinary black-model presence. Certainly, black models were working in the early 1980s, including Iman, the elegant beauty from East Africa who was acclaimed as the first black supermodel. Since then, there have been many firsts among African-American models and consequently much greater exposure. Young women who want to choose a modeling career can see black models on television and in magazines that are not aimed exclusively at black viewers and readers. Tyra has confided her satisfaction in the fact that she has become a role model for young black women:

> When I was young, I used to see all these models and actresses appearing on the pages of fashion magazines, but none of them were my skin tone. I am proud to know that a young lady can leaf through the pages of a magazine and see me in an advertisement, in a photo layout, or in an interview.

Tyra is also aware that models often become sex symbols. She does not object to this view. In 1997, she was chosen for the cover of *Details* magazine's annual issue on sex. When she was asked how she felt about appearing as a sex symbol, she commented: "I'm happy to be a sex symbol. In the modeling industry there have been very few black commercial sex symbols, so I'm glad to break ground." More important to Tyra, however, is the fact that she is striving to change the way African-American women are presented in the media in general. She believes that too often they are shown in a negative way—sexy maybe but as overly seductive vixens. "Black women have always been . . . these animalistic erotic women. Why can't we just be the sexy American girl next door?" she asks.

Some of Tyra's own early experiences have led her to feel strongly about the presence and presentation of African-American women in fashion and advertising. She has taken a stand or made changes where she could, especially when she reached a position to call the shots. When she started out and was looking for modeling agencies, one agent rejected

Wearing a simple but elegant dress and flashing a warm smile, Tyra appears at the Council of Fashion Designers Awards at New York City's Lincoln Center. Tyra saves the haute couture look and her cool demeanor for the runways of the fashion shows.

her because her features were too "ethnic." Another agency told her they already had a black woman and did not want to work with another.

Even in 1991, when she had signed with an agency and had just been chosen for her first major fashion shoot for *Seventeen* magazine, she was taken aback by the attitude of the agency's receptionist. "Tyra, honey," the receptionist said, "you better wipe that cheesy grin off your face. I'll let you know that black models don't have a chance of making it in this industry. So I suggest you come off that cloud you're floating on and learn how to type."

Tyra was not the person to let such discouraging words deter her from her goal of becoming a model. She began working harder than ever and made a special point of being professional and responsible. Tyra seemed to know early on that modeling was a business, and she learned all she could about the fashion industry. All the efforts paid off as she was hired for more and more modeling jobs. Her career really took off when she went to Paris and worked in an unprecedented number of fashion shows. After that, she was ready to choose her jobs carefully and work on her own terms.

For Tyra, working on her own terms has given her the opportunity to speak to other young people about the life she has chosen. She is in great demand as a lecturer in high schools and universities. She shares with her audiences her experiences and aspirations and her goal of changing the image of African-American women in the media.

After speaking at the Volunteerism Awards ceremony, Tyra was surrounded by the many teenagers shyly asking for her autograph. As she signed, she told the young women, "I'm not usually impressed [easily] but I have to say I'm superimpressed today." These teens had undertaken major tasks and had faced great challenges to accomplish what their hearts told them was right. They nodded their heads in agreement when Tyra asserted, "When we volunteer our time and talents to help others, we're the ones who truly benefit." Tyra had not only encouraged young women like them to volunteer but to gain confidence, create skills, work hard, and care for themselves. In doing so, they might one day feel the satisfaction Tyra Banks felt both personally and professionally.

2

YOUNG TYRA

❧

TYRA LYNNE BANKS began her life on her own terms, coming into the world at 7:14 on the evening of December 4, 1973. The baby was named Tyra by her beloved grandmother. At the hospital where Tyra was born, her grandmother heard a long Asian name from a Filipino woman but liked only part of the name. So the second child of Carolyn and Don Banks went home with the "Tyra" part of an Asian name. Home was a cozy house with a play yard in the quiet Los Angeles suburb of Inglewood, California. There, the baby was greeted by her six-year-old brother, Devin, who was excited to welcome the newest member of the family.

In the year of her birth, Tyra's hometown was celebrating its 100th anniversary. Founded in 1873, Inglewood was incorporated as a city in 1908 and grew as a poultry-raising center in its early years. As the Los Angeles metropolitan area expanded, Inglewood changed into an oceanside community. It boasted lovely residential neighborhoods as well as metal, plastics, and furniture industries. By 1967, with the construction of the Great Western Forum sports arena, the city became a well-known sports center. It was home to professional basketball—the Los Angeles Lakers—and hockey—the Los Angeles Kings. The sport of kings—horseracing—also attracted fans to the Hollywood Park racetrack. It was in this

Young Tyra exudes the poise, confidence, and radiant beauty that would propel her to stardom as a supermodel by the time she was 18.

community, five miles from the Pacific Ocean and just south of Los Angeles, Hollywood, and Beverly Hills, that young Tyra Banks grew up.

Don and Carolyn Banks were from Los Angeles and had moved to Inglewood the year Tyra was born. Don Banks was a computer consultant; Carolyn was a medical photographer at NASA's Jet Propulsion Lab. Tyra was part of a close-knit extended family and group of friends. She grew up surrounded by grandparents, great-grandparents, and numerous aunts, uncles, and cousins who were always involved in the family reunions and holidays.

Tyra's childhood was much like that of other kids who are surrounded by a loving family. She played with her cousins and neighborhood children and her brother. She was close to Devin, even though he often played practical jokes on her and teased her because she was awkward and uncoordinated as a child. Nevertheless, he has been one of her best buddies and protectors. "My brother and I have been through it all," she later wrote in her book. " We've shared our low points and our successes. I can't even imagine what my life would be like without having him around."

One of Tyra's favorite memories of her childhood was the abundance of food at the family table. As she wrote, "I was taught to enjoy food, not to fear it." Her grandparents came from Louisiana and Texas, where good food is a necessity and cooking is an art. Tyra remembers how the family kitchen was "always humming at our house. Everywhere I turned there were mouth-watering foods in abundance—fried chicken wings, barbecue ribs, macaroni and cheese, honeyed ham, smothered pork chops, and candied yams. . . ." To this day, Tyra's family always celebrates an event with a grand meal.

As a child, Tyra was an expert at getting her way and wrangling as much attention as she could from adults. And it was her father who most allowed

himself to be wrangled. Tyra was "daddy's little girl," and she knew it. She has admitted that she was badly spoiled. If she could not get her way, all she had to do was fake a few tears, and her wish was instantly granted. It was not her mother, however, who tried to constantly please her daughter. It was Don Banks, for whom his cherished child could do no wrong. She recalled that "We spent a lot of time together. Whatever I wanted to do, he supported it, no matter what the cost."

Later in life, Tyra would remember her privileged childhood. Those memories encouraged her to provide help and support for less fortunate children. As a young child, she was not aware that her life was anything extraordinary. As it turned out, however, she was not immune to her own difficult experience.

Tyra's hometown of Inglewood is the site of the famous Hollywood Park racetrack, which hosts many of the sport's major races. Here, horses streak toward the finish line during the 1997 Breeders' Cup meet.

In 1979, when she was six and Devin was 11, their parents divorced. Fortunately for Tyra and Devin, Don and Carolyn Banks were caring and devoted parents who continued to share parenting roles. Tyra recalls that when her father moved out, she was too young to feel especially hurt or scared. She did, however, sometimes fantasize about getting her parents back together again. It is a tribute to her parents' care and attention that Tyra has not carried terrible emotional scars from the breakup of her family. Don and Carolyn Banks made every effort to minimize the disruption of the divorce and kept their differences from their children. They also knew the importance of making the children's lives as stable as possible.

When her parents separated, Tyra was in a private elementary school, the International Children's School in Los Angeles. Her daily routine didn't change, which helped her adjust to the changes at home. Even her school uniform, a blue jumper with a red-and-white-striped belt, remained the same throughout elementary school. Her father had moved nearby, and she and Devin saw him regularly. Tyra stayed with her mother during the week and saw her father on weekends. She remembers that she was not unhappy with the arrangement. Writing of that period, she recalls: "I had two birthday parties, two Christmases. Double the presents, double the love. As far as I could see, I had it made."

With the passage of time, Tyra also understood that she and Devin and their parents were happier and healthier without the discord that had precipitated the breakup. Communications were open and comfortable. If she ever wondered whether her father still loved her, she could talk to him about it. She has written that ". . . he would reassure me that he would always be there for me and that I'd always be Daddy's little girl. It made me feel ten times better. Expressing yourself really works wonders." From this experience

Tyra learned the importance of open communication and expressing oneself, and she has not hesitated to do so in her adult life.

Tyra also learned early on that exercise was an excellent way to gain reassurance and feel good. Her mother was a strong influence. By the time Tyra was seven, she was watching her mother work out. With her friends, Carolyn exercised to aerobic videos, doing what Tyra calls "nonstop sit-ups" to keep in trim. If the women showed signs of tiring and wanted to stop, Carolyn pushed them on, yelling "No way, honey, keep on going." For Tyra, her mother's youthful figure was proof that having an exercise routine and sticking to it would pay off. With her mother's example before her, Tyra also learned the value of determination and discipline. Tyra recalls, "She was living proof that if I stuck to something, the payoff would be tremendous." Before long, little Tyra was not just observing but participating, making a game of the routine.

As an adult, because keeping her figure and staying healthy are of tremendous importance, Tyra has created her own exercise regimen. Sometimes her workouts are exhilarating, sometimes they are boring, but she has made the decision to keep fit and she has stayed with it. As a child watching her mother sweat and strain to stay in shape, Tyra had learned the value of perseverance.

Tyra also learned another very important lesson about staying healthy. As a little girl, she determined to stay away from tobacco. At the tender age of six, she did try smoking a cigarette. She was at a friend's house playing hide-and-seek when she came upon a cigarette burning in an ashtray. Curious, Tyra grabbed it up and took a big puff, filling her mouth with smoke. She didn't know you were supposed to exhale, and she swallowed the smoke. A scorching pain began in her throat and crept down into her lungs. "After that incident," she said, "I was totally turned

Tyra and her mother, Carolyn, share an affectionate hug. Carolyn has never wavered in her support of her daughter's ambitions. Tyra attributes their closeness to the fact that they have always communicated with each other openly and honestly, even in their disagreements.

off [cigarettes], and to this day, I can't even stand the smell of them."

Although Tyra's one painful episode with a cigarette was short-lived, she and her family were later to experience a far worse emotional pain from the effects of smoking. Her beloved grandmother, Florine London, died of lung cancer at the age of 50. She had been smoking since she was 13. Young Tyra watched as Grandma Florine suffered the cancer's spread throughout her body. "With my grandmother," Tyra says, "I saw up close what habitual smoking can lead to. The images of her last days in the hospital are forever ingrained in my memory. And because of that I told myself I would not promote smoking." Tyra has stayed true to her promise, despite her career in a business that promotes a variety of products, including cigarettes. She will not appear in tobacco ads.

By the time she was nine, Tyra was experiencing her share of such skin problems as extreme dryness and rashes. These problems, however, were minor compared to the warts that developed on both her hands. Coming home from school one day, she threw her books on the table and sobbed. Tears streaked her reddened face as she told her mother the name kids at school were calling her—"Froggy, Froggy!"

Although her parents were sympathetic, they assured her the warts would disappear in time. Months went by, however, and her embarrassment became acute as the warts continued to appear. She wore gloves even in hot weather and hid her hands in her pockets. Finally, after months of crying and whining, she convinced her father something had to be done. He took her to a dermatologist, who froze the warts off her hands. Once again, Tyra had smooth hands, and the gloves came off.

The wart episode had made Tyra self-conscious about her skin. But thanks to her Aunt Sharon, she was able to overcome her feelings. Aunt Sharon convinced Tyra that the warts were not her fault and that she should stop worrying about them. It was her aunt who told her to use her energy taking care of things she could control, such as making sure her skin was soft and healthy. From her aunt, Tyra learned the importance of a healthy skin as part of keeping her health-care regimen.

In that same year, 1983, Tyra faced another issue more difficult than skin problems. This time her trouble was emotional. She faced a difficult adjustment when her mother announced that she was remarrying. Carolyn had met and fallen in love with Clifford Johnson Jr., a high-school graphic arts teacher. Tyra felt as if she had been betrayed and that her stepfather was taking her mother away from her. She tried to put aside her feelings, however, for her mother's sake. In recalling the time, she said, "Instead of whining, sulking, and throwing a tantrum, I put a smile on my face and wished my mom the best of luck."

Despite Tyra's show of acceptance, she was still in conflict over the situation. Johnson was a strict disciplinarian, and he expected Tyra and Devin to follow his direction without questioning. If Tyra's assigned chores, such as washing the dishes, were not done to his satisfaction, she had to do them over. If she was tired or absentminded and left her clothes lying around, her stepfather would wake her from her sleep, if necessary, to put them away. She compared his authoritarianism to her mother's more relaxed attitude. Carolyn would complain but she let her daughter get away with things. Tyra resented Johnson's strictness and looked upon him as a bully who loved giving orders.

Because of her resentment, Tyra did not always appreciate her stepfather's positive qualities. She admitted that he was always there when she needed someone to talk to. He would stop what he was doing and listen to her. She also began to realize his talents as an artist and was grateful for his help in her school projects. She began to see him as an individual who genuinely cared for her, and she learned to communicate with him. "I had to allow myself to meet my stepfather halfway," she said. "Just that little step took our relationship forward by leaps and bounds."

Tyra was growing up. The insights she eventually brought to her relationship with her family would help her continue to grow emotionally and socially. As she entered adolescence and faced new challenges, she was developing the persistence and determination that would carry her through the next 10 years. At the end of those years, she would find herself still surrounded by a loving, supportive family but surprisingly independent as she pursued her chosen career.

3

"DON'T EVER LET ANYONE TELL YOU, YOU CAN'T DO SOMETHING"

T YRA BANKS'S EARLY teenage years were for the most part unexceptional. She grew physically, learned more about the world, and began to discover who and what she wanted to be. At the same time, her perception of herself changed radically. How did she view herself and how would that view affect her future? Had she been able to look ahead, she would have seen that the steps she took were somewhat surprising and certainly fortunate.

In 1984, Tyra graduated from elementary school and entered John Burroughs Middle School in Los Angeles. For Tyra, however, the school's large campus proved to be intimidating. Used to small classes in elementary school, she was uncomfortable and overwhelmed. Two years later, she transferred to the all-girls Immaculate Heart Middle and High School. At first, she was not sure whether she liked the idea of going to school with only girls. In a short time, however, she realized the advantages of Immaculate Heart. "We didn't worry about looking 'cute' and styling our hair and makeup for hours to impress guys," she remembered. "We concentrated on our schoolwork and campus events." Tyra was also impressed with the fact that girls were in leadership positions in student government and sports. Tyra's experience at Immaculate Heart helped open her eyes to the fact that young women could be strong and independent.

Tyra did not let anyone tell her she could not succeed as a model. From an awkward, often insecure teen, she transformed her tall, leggy frame into the image of a poised, self-confident young woman.

Before going to Immaculate Heart, Tyra entered what she has called the "awkward" age, and she remembers it as a time she would not want to relive. Over a period of only three months she grew three inches and at the same time lost 20 pounds. She was taller than most of her classmates, and before she turned 12 she towered over them and her teacher as well. She was 5'9" tall and thin as a rail.

Concerned that Tyra had a medical disorder, her mother took her to several doctors. All pronounced her perfectly healthy and assured Tyra and her mother that she was fine. She would, they said, eventually gain weight. For Tyra, however, it seemed as if her body was betraying her and was completely beyond her control.

The girl who had once been an extrovert with scores of friends, who clowned in class, now became a freak in her own eyes. She felt she was nothing but a tall, skinny stick in a girl's body. She was self-conscious and miserable. Unable to look people in the eye, she avoided friendly gazes and rude stares alike in fear of teasing comments. She remembers such remarks as "Gosh, she's so skinny she'd blow over if a big wind came along," and "Quick, somebody give her a pork chop." Sometimes she was taunted with names like "Olive Oyl" and "Lightbulb Head" because her head seemed so large on such a thin body. She spent much of her time locked in her room.

In an effort to gain weight, Tyra gobbled up the most fattening foods she could find. She remembers some of the artery-clogging dishes she concocted: "I'd make myself chocolate-and-peanut butter ice cream shakes every night before bedtime. But nothing seemed to work. I'd get on the scale every day, but my weight stayed the same. Ninety-eight pounds."

Although Tyra finally gained weight, it did not happen overnight. As a early teenager, she saw the girls around her developing curves as they became young women. Her body, however, remained the same, "straight and narrow." Finally, around the age of 17, Tyra's body began to fill out as she gained weight. That was the time when she finally felt good about her figure. Later, when as a sought-after model her figure had acquired alluring curves, she did not look like so many of the other thin, nearly anorexic models who appeared to be the standard in the profession. Tyra does not deny herself the food she likes: french fries, ribs, ice cream. "I don't starve myself," she has said. "I don't really diet at all. Letting go a little is my way of saying to other women, 'Don't let fashion make you insecure.'"

As if growing tall and losing weight were not enough to diminish her self-image, Tyra also had to wear braces on her teeth and later she needed glasses. Despite her discomfort with her appearance during her early teenage years, Tyra did gain more self-confidence at this time. She enjoyed the usual teen experimenting and pranks. At 13, she was unhappy with her sandy-brown hair; she wanted to have jet-black hair like her best friend. Her mother had told her she could not even think of dyeing her hair until she was 16. But Tyra went to a hairdresser anyway, telling her it was okay to change her hair color. When her mother saw the change, she punished Tyra by grounding her for a month.

The next year, she began dating a young man she had met at a Bobby Brown concert. He was 18, and she told him she was 17. When her parents found out, Tyra was forbidden to see him. She tried to sneak out and meet him and was caught. She lost her phone and dating privileges, and that was the end of that.

Tyra enjoyed the company of her many friends. One in particular helped her make a choice that would greatly affect her adult lifestyle. One day, when she was 13, Tyra was hanging out at a friend's house and was offered a glass of peach wine cooler. She took a sip and knew immediately she did not like it. Tyra was aware that her friend drank, often becoming nearly unconscious. She asked her friend why she drank something that did not even taste good and left a terrible aftertaste. The girl agreed but said that drinking made her feel good. Tyra decided that she would not drink then or as an adult. From that time on, she has found it easy to turn down alcohol. Tyra's youthful resolve was one more step on the way to becoming the person the future Tyra Banks would be. She would be a person who was in control of her life.

In 1987, Tyra entered Immaculate Heart High School and at 15, she began stepping out a bit. Thanks to the support of her mother and her many school friends, she exchanged her early insecurities for a tentative poise that fitted her tall frame. At least being thin, rather than heavy, gave her more clothing options. With encouragement, she began dressing up her lean body and gained a new sense of style. On school days, she still had to don a uniform, which as she remembered gave a minimal choice of styles. "We could choose between two skirts, either gray wool in winter or yellow cotton in the spring, alternate between three shirt colors (blue, yellow, or white), and wear either penny loafers or oxfords." On weekends, Tyra wrapped herself in her comfortable at-home uniform—blue jeans and a white T-shirt.

One of Tyra's friends, Khefri Riley, was quite into fashion. She persuaded Tyra that she was really attractive, especially when she dressed up. Led by Khefri and another friend, Robyn Roth, Tyra began frequenting thrift shops to find wardrobe treasures. They had a routine of creating inexpensive outfits that reflected their own developing personal style.

Tyra's mother was especially creative when it came to matters of clothes. When Tyra was in elementary school, there was a free-dress day once a

Young Tyra favored outfits like this oversize shirt and baggy overalls. When, as a supermodel, she wore many of the world's most exclusive fashions, she still loved her "bummy" clothes. "I feel comfortable in these clothes," she said. "This is the way I dress and look."

Browsing through thrift shops like this, Tyra and her friends spent hours looking for just the right clothes to make inexpensive outfits. Choosing her own clothes gave Tyra a sense of independence and the chance to create her own personal style.

month. No uniforms were required. She and her classmates would scramble to find just the right outfit. All wanted to outshine one another. Tyra would pick out something new she wanted, and her mother would find something similar and cheaper and buy it for her. By the time Tyra was in high school and ready for her senior prom, her mother brought in a seamstress to recreate Tyra's chosen style. Carolyn thoroughly enjoyed advising her daughter. As a photographer, she had an eye for lines and proportions and usually photographed their joint fashion successes.

As a child, Tyra had enjoyed dressing up in her mother's heels and long dresses and playing at being a model. That, however, had been just a child pretending. Being a real model had not been a serious childhood dream. And despite her enjoyment as a teen in selecting and wearing various fashions and being photographed, Tyra had to be persuaded to try modeling. Her friend Khefri, who had already signed with an agency, urged Tyra to make a stab at it. For a year, Khefri badgered her friend. Eventually, she wore Tyra down. In 1989, Tyra made a decision. She would look for an agency.

Tyra was optimistic as she began making the rounds, starting with her friend's agency. Her mother, who had shot the photos for Tyra's portfolio, accompanied the young hopeful. Tyra's confidence turned to disappointment, however, as she encountered rejection after rejection. Agencies already had someone like her, or she did not have the look they wanted. One agency looked at her photos for less than a minute and turned her down. Discouraged, she decided to try one more agency. She described what happened:

> I walked in, handed my photos to the secretary, and waited for what seemed like hours. Finally, one of the agents came to the front office to meet me. She sat down in front of me and said, "Well, Tyra, I see that you have some potential. But I'm only going to have you do runway shows, because I don't feel that the camera likes your face."

Despite the agent's lack of enthusiasm, Tyra signed with the outfit—L.A. Models. Her family was solidly behind her as she took her first career steps. As she has said, "My parents were very supportive from the beginning. They respected my choice to give modeling a try. . . ." Her mother's admonition "Don't ever let anyone tell you, you can't do something" certainly encouraged her to push ahead.

Just getting a foot in the door was a start. Although

it was a tentative beginning, it was better than none at all. Tyra vowed that she would show the agent whose face the camera liked. And indeed, within three years, Tyra would be supporting herself on the huge sums of money that designers, agencies, and a cosmetics company would pay for the privilege of presenting her face to the public.

After signing with the agency, Tyra had to begin juggling schoolwork, small modeling jobs, and her social life. She took both school and modeling very seriously and neither suffered. In fact, Tyra applied the same work ethic to both jobs.

> Just like someone would study for a class, I studied the different aspects of modeling. I continued to do photo sessions until I improved. I continued walking until I was good enough to go onto a runway. I learned to do my own makeup so that I would not have to depend on the makeup artists all the time. I studied my face in the mirror. I didn't take anything for granted. *I was prepared.*

In 1990, Tyra signed with a different agency, Elite Model Management, where she was accepted, if not overly encouraged. She also worked hard to finish high school. After graduation, she wanted to continue her education in college and already knew she would major in film and television production. Modeling gave her some money, and she liked the work. But she did not think of it as a permanent substitute for the "real" life she was planning.

Tyra plowed through exams and then sifted through college brochures. Finally she applied to the five schools that she and her family liked best: Loyola Marymount University in Los Angeles, the University of California at Los Angeles, the University of Southern California, New York University, and California State University at Los Angeles.

Events were moving swiftly now. The school year was winding down, and Tyra was accepted at Loyola

Marymount, her first choice. Good-byes and new beginnings loomed on the horizon. Some awkward and challenging years were behind her, and she was full of confidence for the future. Tyra was ready for the larger world she expected to enter. Like a newly hatched butterfly, she had been transformed and was now ready to try her wings. Inside, Tyra had matured as well. She was stronger and more determined than ever to prove herself. She would soon have that opportunity, although not the one she had anticipated.

4

IN THE SPOTLIGHT:
A YEAR IN PARIS

❦

EVENTS OF THE year 1991 completely changed the life of 17-year-old Tyra Banks. In one 12-month period, she set out on a new path, beginning a career she could not have imagined. Only a short time later, she would be well established in her profession and on her own at the age of 20.

It had all begun in 1990 when as a high-school senior, she was selected by *Seventeen* magazine to be photographed for an upcoming issue. An editor at the magazine had been calling agencies in Los Angeles, looking for new models. When Tyra's agent at the time, L.A. Models, sent some of Tyra's photos, the editor was impressed. She saw a tall, beautiful girl who looked like she was enjoying herself immensely. The young model was hired on the spot, and *Seventeen*'s crew went to Los Angeles to meet her. Tyra was photographed for the March 1991 issue of the magazine. When the issue was published, teachers at Immaculate Heart posted a sign on the bulletin board. It read: "Congratulations on being in *Seventeen* magazine!"

The *Seventeen* photos were just the beginning, although Tyra was not aware of it at the time. With high school behind her, she was in the summer of 1991 spending time with friends, working, and preparing for college. Then, only two weeks before she was to enter Loyola Marymount, her plans

Tyra's signature stroll down the runways of Paris fashion shows helped catapult her into stardom as a model. Following her success in Paris, she never looked back.

abruptly changed. Her agency, now Elite Model Management, introduced her to a representative from a French modeling agency, which offered to sponsor her for a year to model at the *haute couture* shows in Paris. Fashion moves by seasons, as designers present their new apparel in the fall/winter and the spring/summer seasons. Tyra would be participating in the fall/winter 1991 season and stay for the 1992 spring/summer shows. Her heart racing, Tyra accepted the extraordinary chance to live and work in the fashion capital of the world.

Paris was the home of countless models, designers, and agencies. If Tyra wanted to be in the modeling world, this was her chance. She and her family quickly changed gears. Books were put aside for the time being, and Loyola Marymount gave her a year's deferment. Carolyn Johnson fully supported her daughter's decision, coaching her and helping her prepare for the runway shows Tyra would be part of in Paris. Tyra studied international fashion shows by renting videos from the Fashion Design Institute. She spent hours watching Cindy Crawford on MTV's *House of Style* and Elsa Klensch on CNN's *Style*. Wearing her mother's high heels and long nightgowns, she paraded back in forth in the living room while her mother gave advice and tips. Tyra recalls that "My ankles would shake and I would bend my knees and stick my lips out."

One of the most important items Tyra needed was a really sensational model's photo portfolio to show to designers and print agencies in Paris. Here, Carolyn's expertise was essential. Once again, she began photographing her daughter, shooting her in a variety of poses. Before Tyra knew it, she had modeled her way to a full portfolio of poses: *Tyra innocent, Tyra sophisticated, Tyra come hither*. Thanks to Carolyn it was all there—the beauty, the charisma, the versatility. In September, Tyra was on the plane to Paris.

Barefoot, a little wide-eyed, the young model is "Tyra innocent" in one of the portfolio shots that helped convince Paris designers and agents that Tyra was ready for the world of fashion.

The Eiffel Tower, symbol of Paris, looms over the city. Often lonely in the "City of Light," Tyra learned to appreciate its many famous attractions and to enjoy them on her own as she gained a new sense of independence.

Tyra found Paris fascinating. She encountered new people, a new culture, and a new language. She walked the streets soaking up the ambience, looking in windows, and watching other people. For Tyra, however, what was different and unique about Paris was also a source of homesickness and frustration. It was hard for her to adjust to a foreign place. She knew hardly anyone there except her agents and a few models, and she was often very lonely. When asked years later about her earliest memories of modeling experiences, she would still answer, "Being lonely in Paris in a model's apartment the size of a breadbox and being extremely homesick with no friends or family around."

Although Tyra found a way to learn from her experience, she first had to overcome her longing for home. Food was her answer. She listed the names of all the American fast-food places in Paris and proceeded to eat her way through them. Each day she visited one of them—a McDonald's, a Haagen-Daz, a Burger King. She entreated her mother to send her junk food from home. She led Carolyn to believe these were just snacks. In reality, they were her main meals. She was, she recalled, "eating sandwich cookies for breakfast, peanut brittle for lunch, and caramel corn for dinner." She was so lacking in nutrition that at one fashion show she nearly fainted on the runway.

Gradually, Tyra got over her food obsession. Equally important, she learned how to navigate Paris by herself—in her own words she was "solo socializing"—and explore the city's many wonderful attractions. The young woman who had admitted that she often felt uncomfortable being alone took up the challenge of going it on her own. Uninterested in Paris nightlife or the party scene, she discovered new pleasures.

Tyra visited museums, found restaurants that served good French food, frequented American bookstores, and looked for films with English subtitles. She found she really liked shopping in the small grocery stores, butcher shops, and especially the bakeries where she loved to inhale the delicious smells from the ovens. She talked with tourists at sidewalk cafes and even practiced some French with shopkeepers. It did not take Tyra long to realize that she could find a great deal of pleasure spending time alone.

The first time Tyra's mother visited her in Paris, she was completely surprised by her daughter's spirit of independence and what she had learned on her own. Tyra was indeed beginning to feel comfortable with, and even proud of, her newly acquired self-reliance. In remembering her early experience in Paris, she says "[It] made me aware of my true inner strengths and helped me to hone my survival skills. . . . It taught me to learn about myself, to ask myself questions like: 'Who am I?' 'What is my philosophy of life?' 'What truly makes me happy?'"

Professionally, Tyra found immediate success in Paris. She made the rounds of designer showrooms and magazine offices, usually dressed in her favorite clothes—blue jeans and a white T-shirt. Such an outfit might seem inappropriate for interviews. However, the world of fashion is not like other professions. Tyra later explained, "I guess my bummy fashion approach set me apart from the crowd and made a big impression on the designers." She learned from this experience that fashion is not a question of buying the newest and fanciest clothes. If you put your own personal stamp on your fashions, that is what makes you unique.

What is also tremendously important in the world of fashion is a model's portfolio. Agents and designers learn a lot about a model just from her photos. How does she look in different moods? different

Tyra glides confidently down the runway at a Ralph Lauren show. Lauren, who consistently used black models in his shows, was only one of the several top designers for whom Tyra modeled in Paris.

styles? different environments? How versatile is she? In Tyra agents saw potential right away. Within two weeks of arriving in Paris, she had her first magazine cover when the French magazine *20 Ans* (Twenty-Year-Old) snapped her up for a shoot. Under bright studio lights, the *20 Ans* camera caught her lithe figure in a black-trimmed red jacket and pants. Within a month, her picture looked out at passersby from the newsstands. Surrounded by "reader teasers"— the blurbs on magazine covers that tempt readers to buy—her image presented a young woman of both innocence and alluring beauty.

Tyra's look captivated the fashion world. That fall she was invited to the runways of some of the world's most prestigious designers. Karl Lagerfeld, Yves Saint Laurent, Oscar de la Renta, and Chanel all vied for her appearance. In a six-day period, she appeared on 25 runways, an unprecedented record for a newcomer. Time after time, she strode down the long runways under the hot lights. Her smile and natural exuberance delighted audiences. On one walk, she might wear an elegant suit; on another, she might appear in a fluffy confection. By the end of a show, Tyra could have changed her outfit several times.

What was it that made Tyra such a sought-after model? Her awesome, willowy height and unique stroll were part of it. One magazine described her demeanor: "Her sensual lope and sleek, space-age frame gave her instant catwalk [runway] charisma." Model Niki Taylor described her as a "live wire" who had an unbelievable presence on the runway. And designer Todd Oldham compared Tyra to a beautiful animal. He said that she was like "an antelope. She was just born with grace."

Young Tyra Banks's stint in Paris was a turning point in her life. Beautiful, energetic, disciplined, and hardworking, she had won acclaim and was ready to pursue the career that would lead to incredible fame and fortune. She had gone to Paris as a high-school graduate and would return home as fashion's latest hot item. Although she was to be a "first" in several facets of modeling, she was not the first African-American woman to reach the heights in the fashion world. Others had come before, easing the way for young women like Tyra.

5

TRANSCENDING THE
COLOR BARRIER

❧

IN MARCH 1997 designer Jean Paul Gaultier staged a show in Paris that excited the fashion world. As designers, retailers, and advertising people watched, models appeared through billowing clouds of smoke to emerge onto the runway. It was not the traditional catwalk but was made to look like a boxing ring. To the surprise of the viewers, most of the models were black.

The show was Gaultier's salute to black fashion style, from the glamour of the 1920s through the "soul" of the 1970s and into the hip-hop flavor of the 1990s. Red, green, and yellow "flapper" dresses and fur-trimmed coats recalled the Harlem of the 1920s; black leather pants topped by hooded sweatshirts symbolized the era of hip-hop. Many of the fabrics were the traditional cloths woven in Africa. Hairdos ranged from the flat, waved style of the 1920s to the huge Afros of the 1970s and 1980s. The show was one of the big hits of the season.

Only a few years earlier, such an array of African-American models in a show that saluted black-fashion heritage would have been nearly unthinkable. It took many years of determination and dedication for African-American models, and those who supported them, to break the color barrier.

In 1955, the *New York Post* estimated that about 250 black models were working in New York City.

In the 1960s and 1970s, African-American models appeared on the fashion runways but were nearly invisible in magazines or in advertising. An exception was Jackie Clay, who often modeled for magazines in the 1960s.

Walking on New York City's Fifth Avenue, Naomi Sims heads for a modeling assignment. One of the most celebrated models of her time, Sims left a lasting legacy when she opened the modeling doors for African-American women.

The newspaper reported that most of these were part-timers who modeled almost exclusively for African-American magazines and advertisers. Then, in 1956 a crack appeared in the wall of what one designer called "fashion apartheid." A dark-skinned Eurasian beauty, China Machado, began working in Paris as a house model for Givenchy. She was invited to New York, where she appeared in a fashion show and was extensively photographed. In 1959, when a photographer wanted to picture her in *Bazaar* magazine's fashion collections as their first nonwhite model, the publisher refused. However, the magazine later relented. Machado continued modeling until

1962, when she became a senior editor at *Bazaar*.

During the 1960s African-American models began to become more visible. The civil rights movement, with its emphasis on equality and economic opportunity, helped open doors for black models. At the same time, as more black designers were gaining a toehold in the fashion world, opportunities appeared for models of color. The fashion industry was eager for anything new, different, and exotic. Money, of course, played an important role. If millions could be made by featuring African-American models, designers and advertisers would not turn this money down. Still, black figures did not often appear on runways, in showrooms, or in the pages of mainstream "white" magazines.

After the assassination of Martin Luther King Jr., a young woman named Katiti Kironde II made headlines of a sort when she appeared on the cover of the August 1968 issue of *Glamour*. She was the first African-American to appear on the cover of a major fashion magazine. According to Jerry Ford of the Ford Modeling Agency, "The death of King shook everybody a bit and woke them up to the fact that something had to be done."

Then in 1969 a woman who would make a lasting impression on the fashion industry burst upon the scene. Naomi Sims, described by one writer as "a mahogany-skinned beauty with high cheekbones, wide, pointed nose, and full lips," made the breakthrough when she was featured on the cover of *Life* magazine. Sims, who at that point was earning $1,000 a week from various modeling assignments, later appeared in *Vogue* and on the cover of the *Ladies' Home Journal*. Even after appearing in several prestigious magazines, Sims still had trouble getting any top agency in New York to represent her because they did not think they could get enough work for a black model. The Cooper agency finally did sign her on, and Sims went on to become a very well-known model in the late 1960s and early 1970s. When she retired she opened a business offering wigs and cosmetics tailored for black women and authored an autobiography telling of her struggle and accomplishments in the world of fashion.

During the 1970s several African-American models rose to prominence. Among them were Peggy Dillard and Barbara Smith, the first black women to appear on the cover of *Mademoiselle*. In 1974, a champion swimmer from Buffalo, New York, Beverly Johnson, made the cover of American *Vogue*. Her appearance was *Vogue's* first for a black model. Still, it was easier for African-American women to appear on the runways of the Paris fashion shows than on the runways of New York. French designer Givenchy used many black models during the 1970s. When questioned about his choices, he explained that when he went to Los Angeles to present his shows, black women were the only good models he could find. When he was criticized for using so many young black women, he responded that he was not concerned about what people thought. "I got a lot of inspiration from the models," he said.

American designers finally caught on and began hiring African-American models. Among them was Ralph Lauren, who had many black women walking his runways. However, he did not often use them in his advertisements. In the early 1970s it was still difficult for black models to appear in magazines. It was one thing to display fashions on the runway for a limited audience and another to appeal to the readers of mainstream magazines or gain lucrative contracts to advertise products. Designers blamed agents for not sending them black models, and agents and advertisers blamed designers for not asking for black women.

Still, prominent African-American models eventually made the crossover. Among them was the woman sometimes called the High Priestess of

Iman, the first black supermodel, poses with Peter Beard, the photographer who discovered her in Kenya. She led the way for other black models when she achieved success, and international fame, on both the fashion runways and in print.

fashion. Iman, the lovely model from Africa, was discovered by a photographer in the mid-1970s when she was a student at the University of Nairobi in Kenya. Iman is a native of Somalia, which is predominantly a Muslim nation where women do not have the same advantages as men. Her parents, especially her mother, a doctor, taught Iman that she had choices and could be as good as any man.

A storm of publicity followed her discovery. Her exotic beauty, cool demeanor, and elegant walk brought her international fame and made her one of the most sought-after models of the 1970s. She was also one of the highest paid, receiving as much as $100,000 for modeling one collection.

When asked about what appears to be her "grand attitude," one designer has commented that behind the facade she is a true professional who is also "the perfect model. She gives expression to the clothes." Of her tremendous appeal and success, Iman has commented: "I'm a . . . black model, succeeding in a country that craves blonde, blue-eyed teenagers. I've taken work away from blonde women. I've even taken work away from men. I'm secure within myself—independent, a survivor."

When Revlon hired Iman as a spokesperson for one of its cosmetic lines, she became one of the first black models to promote products for a major firm. In the mid-1980s, Iman retired from modeling and moved easily into films and television. She appeared in cameo roles in films that included *Out of Africa*, *No Way Out*, and *Star Trek VI*, and made TV appearances on the *Cosby Show* and *In the Heat of the Night*. She wants to expand her acting career in the future and is interested in making videos. In 1997, designer Donna Karan asked Iman to come out of retirement in modeling to star in her spring advertising campaign.

Another prominent African-American model is Naomi Campbell, one of today's most famous

Naomi Campbell's slightly Asian look, which she inherited from a Chinese grandmother, gives her beauty a special quality. She has been filmed on locations around the world, including a shoot during which she perched on the edge of a volcano.

supermodels, who is blessed with stunning good looks and irrepressible charm. Discovered in London at the age of 15, Campbell appears in fashion magazines such as *Vogue*, *Cosmopolitan*, and *Elle*, and is constantly in demand on the runways of North America and Europe. Fashion photographers enthuse over Campbell's grace and elegance. "No one else has such an amazing body. She makes clothes come alive," says one photographer.

Although Campbell has branched out into films and television, she primarily focuses on modeling for now. Campbell does not want to be categorized as a "black" model. And her wish has come true as attitudes are changing. As she has said: "They used to call up asking for a beautiful white model or a beautiful black model. Now they just ask for a beautiful model. It just doesn't matter what color you are anymore. If I've had anything to do with that change, then I'm really proud."

Veronica Webb is another model who, like Iman, broke down barriers when she signed a multi-million-dollar contract with Revlon. She became a cosmetics spokesperson for the company in 1992. One of the supermodels, Webb has been described as "more than a pretty face on legs-up-to-here. She's got a mind that's sharper than the claws at a table of ladies who lunch. And she's not above getting in her licks." She is known in the fashion world as a young woman of great intelligence and business sense. She conducted most of the negotiations for the Revlon contract herself.

Growing up in Detroit, Michigan, Webb did not have ambitions to become a model. She was a gifted artist and thought she might become an animator. She was encouraged by her parents to be independent and achieve what she wanted on her own merit. After being "discovered" working in a boutique in New York City and encouraged to become a model, Webb modeled in fashion shows in Paris and New York.

Like Tyra Banks, Webb is a woman of diverse talents. She is a recognized journalist who contributes magazine articles on such issues as AIDS, abortion, sexual harassment, and birth control for teens. As an actress she has appeared in Spike Lee's films *Jungle Fever* and *Malcolm X*. Aware of the uncertainties of modeling, Webb has carved out a multifaceted career and has enjoyed a variety of

Tyra, at left, shares the spotlight with Veronica Webb, who broke a color barrier in the modeling world when she signed a lucrative contract as model and spokesperson for Revlon. Like Tyra, Webb is a multitalented woman. She has assured her future by becoming a highly successful journalist and actor.

experiences. As she has said: "In order to live in America, I had to diversify because as a black model there was nowhere else to go." Veronica Webb is a confident, self-assured woman who, as one writer said, is a "role model of black beauty."

Following in Tyra's own footsteps, another young black woman who has attained supermodel status is 21-year-old Alek Wek. A native of the Sudan, in Africa, she and her family fled their war-torn country and settled in London. Wek has a radically different look from the more European features of some of her black contemporaries. Like Tyra, she is a tall 5′11″, but her skin color is a shiny ebony and she does not straighten her hair but wears it natural and closely cropped. Wek has appeared on the runways of Paris, New York, and Milan, Italy, where she has been described as a model whose "happy personality wears the clothes." She has also had cameo roles in Janet Jackson and Busta Rhymes music videos, which have made her popular on MTV.

As the fashion industry promotes her African look, controversy has flared up. Many applaud the industry's acceptance of more "blackness" in fashion models. Some African Americans, however, feel that Wek is presented as a stereotype of what white Americans think of blacks—that is, full lips, wide nose, and dark black hair. Others, however, especially young women, respond favorably to Wek's look. When she appeared on the cover of *Elle* magazine, the magazine received more positive mail than it had ever received for any other cover. Wek herself does not quite understand what the fuss is about. "In my village there is no problem because we all look the same. Here there is so much difference in skin— so much is thought about it, and that's sad," she commented.

Tyra Banks has certainly benefited from the changes in attitudes about African-American models. She is more likely, however, to agree with Veronica Webb than with Naomi Campbell, who had asserted that color does not matter anymore. "I think it's [still] a struggle," said Tyra, "and I'm glad I have a large part in breaking those barriers." In fact, Tyra's role models include Iman, 1984 Miss America Vanessa Williams, as well as white models Cindy Crawford and Claudia Schiffer, whom she admires for their perseverance and professionalism.

There is probably some rivalry between Tyra and Naomi Campbell. Early in her career, Tyra was often referred to as the "new Naomi Campbell." Campbell can be temperamental, and reportedly she was angry at the comparison. She refused to speak to Tyra on several occasions and through her influence got Tyra barred from a Chanel show. "It's very sad," Tyra lamented, "that the fashion business and press [as well as certain other models] can't accept that there can be more than one reigning black super-model at a time." She noted that to be successful, she should not have to edge out Naomi Campbell.

Many changes have occurred in the way that the fashion industry and the media present the beauty of African-American women. Much of this progress has been the result of the perseverance of women like Tyra and her predecessors. Their determination to face challenges and overcome them has allowed the once exotic in fashion to become simply and properly just another expression of beauty.

When Tyra Banks was asked what it was like for her to have achieved so many "firsts" in the world of modeling, she responded: "I have been fortunate in my career to be able to transcend long-standing barriers. I hope and realize that my success . . . is paving the way for other 'firsts' to be achieved until there is no longer a need for the distinction."

6

MOVING UP:
"YOU GO, GIRL"

&

PARIS HAD SPREAD Tyra's name and image throughout the fashion community. She had matured, becoming her own person and experiencing the ups and downs of life in the fashion industry. As the time came to return home in October 1992, she had two goals in mind. She was determined to create a scholarship at her former high school for young African-American women, and she wanted to set up her own corporation.

She was not yet 19 years old when she founded the Tyra Banks Scholarship for African-American girls at Immaculate Heart. A year later, in 1993, she established Ty Girl Corporation (which later was renamed Bankable, Inc.). Knowing her family supported her ambitions, she wanted them around her. She urged her mother, who had closely watched and guided her daughter's budding career, to quit her job and become Tyra's full-time manager. Tyra convinced her father to handle her financial affairs, and she hired a cousin to handle her abundance of fan mail. Despite her new-found independence, Tyra still relied heavily on family support, especially that of her mother. The youthful model had always looked up to Carolyn as her strongest role model. The values of discipline, hard work, and persistence were Carolyn's legacy to her daughter.

As soon as Tyra arrived home from Paris, the

Moving up in the fashion world gave Tyra the opportunity to reach one of her cherished goals, establishing a scholarship for African-American girls at her alma mater, Immaculate Heart. She enjoys a happy moment with school principal Ruth Anne Murray as she presents a donation to the scholarship fund.

offers began pouring in. She plunged into her work, focusing her full attention on her modeling career. With her growing recognition came a whirlwind schedule. Travel was a hectic necessity as she flew to magazine and advertising shoots and fashion shows across the country and overseas. Tyra became a familiar presence in New York, Paris, Milan, and London. Her image graced the covers of such magazines as *Cosmopolitan*, *Vogue*, *Elle*, *Esquire*, and *Harper's Bazaar*.

Although Tyra was endowed with youthful energy, travel often wore her down. "The endless travel is hard sometimes," she admitted. "Being alone in hotel rooms all over the world can be very lonely—thank God for the telephone."

Fashion shows and magazine shoots were just the beginning, however. In 1993, Tyra netted a lucrative modeling contract with a major cosmetics company, Cover Girl. She agreed to be a high-profile model and spokesperson for the company, doing print and television advertisements. The contract was exclusive; she could not model for other similar businesses. Tyra was the third African-American woman to sign such a contract.

Appearing for Cover Girl is a coveted position in the world of models. The woman who signs with a cosmetics firm is considered to have "arrived." Being seen on television commercials and in print ads very often propels cosmetic-company models into stardom. Earlier Cover Girl models such as Cheryl Tiegs and Christie Brinkley became household names. And young models such as Lucy Gordon, Jua Perez, Sarah Thomas, and Carrie Tivador, all of whom signed with Cover Girl in 1997, hope to achieve the stardom Tyra did after signing with the company. Such recognition also translates into further work.

For Tyra, 1993 was also a breakthrough year in another arena. She landed a recurring role in the popular NBC television sitcom *The Fresh Prince of*

Bel-Air. She played the athletic, spirited college student Jackie Ames, the former girlfriend of the show's "Fresh Prince," Will Smith. To get the part, Tyra first rehearsed at home under her mother's direction. Then, in a replay of her Paris auditions, she presented herself to the producers dressed in a T-shirt and athletic shoes. The producers were impressed. It also helped that her 5'11" frame was a good match for 6'2" Will Smith.

Tyra thoroughly enjoyed the role of Jackie, and her acting talents were well received. Filmmaker John Singleton, who directed the acclaimed *Boyz 'n the Hood* and *Rosewood*, also took notice of the budding actor. "Tyra is good," he said. "She adds a lot of flavor to what could have been a throwaway role."

Tyra also discovered that being in television makes her more accessible as a public figure. She describes how people she meets react to her television image:

> When people know me as a model they back off. They have trouble relating to the image they see in the magazines. But when they recognize me from television, they relate to me as this chill-out girl. It's like, "Hey girl, what's up?"

Throughout her career, Tyra has continued her charity work, sponsoring fundraisers and promoting causes dear to her heart, including participating in AIDS awareness projects. At the end of 1993, she had a wrenching personal experience involving a man named Theo, who was dying of AIDS. Tyra learned through her mother that Theo was a fan. She had never visited one-on-one with an AIDS patient, and she wanted to meet Theo.

Tyra was apprehensive at first, but not about the AIDS. She wondered what she and Theo would talk about and what she could say to him. Theo put her at ease immediately, and for three hours, they laughed and joked together. He made her smile when he complimented her on her looks. She

Tyra gives a great deal of time and effort to causes she sponsors. Here, she loads up her plate at a barbecue given for the Pediatric AIDS Foundation, one of her cherished projects.

thought she looked like a monster without her makeup and with her hair uncombed. As Tyra recorded in her diary, it was an evening she would always remember.

Theo died shortly after her visit, but Tyra has not forgotten him and the few moments of happiness they shared. She later wrote: "He opened my eyes, not only to AIDS, but to our shared humanity. He may have thought meeting me was special, but I'm the one who will always be grateful for meeting him."

In 1994, Tyra had the opportunity to make the transition from television to films. Although she had enjoyed the role of Jackie Ames in *Fresh Prince* and liked the public recognition, she did not want to be stereotyped into the Ames character. When an offer came to take a role in a movie by John Singleton, the same director who had seen her and praised her talents, she did not hesitate. In fact, Singleton had seen her earlier at a fashion show in Los Angeles and was smitten by her beauty and grace on the runway.

In Singleton's film *Higher Learning*, Tyra portrays Deja, a student and track runner at a university. The film features, among other stars, Ice Cube, Jennifer Connelly, and Laurence Fishburne. Tyra liked the theme of the movie, which explores stereotyping and racial tensions among first-semester freshmen students. She also got to express a part of her own personality as she constantly urges her boyfriend in the film to "Use what you have to get what you want."

As it turned out, Tyra's biggest challenge was not the acting but the intense athletics required. As she explained, "Usually people have a couple of *months* to prepare for a movie. I had to learn to hurdle in three weeks. . . . I was running so much that I lost twelve to fifteen pounds." It was, however, her acting ability that surprised critics, who apparently expected less from a model.

It was during the filming of *Higher Learning* that Tyra and John Singleton began dating. When Singleton first told her he wanted them to date only each other, she hesitated. She did not want to rush their romance. Later, she agreed and told him she "wanted to be his girl." She would not agree, however, to live with Singleton. "Not until I get married," she said. "I'm old fashioned."

Being in a film was a challenge but an enjoyable one, and Tyra was looking forward to doing more movies. When an interviewer asked what kinds of roles she would like, she replied: "I don't just want to be the bimbo. . . . I want a meaty role, like an addict or a *femme fatale*. I'd love to be the villain." Although Tyra feels she would enjoy such roles, she did turn down a chance to play a seductress in the

In one of three guest-star appearances on Fox TV's New York Undercover, Tyra played a sexy French teacher who falls in love with Malik Yoba's character, J.C., an undercover cop.

Tom Cruise film *The Firm*. When asked why, she responded that she wanted her roles to be more than decorative: "I don't want roles that scream, 'I am so pretty.'"

Until another film opportunity came along, however, Tyra added more credits to her multifaceted career and further enhanced her image as a role model. She began accepting offers to lecture to young people. In 1995 the University of Texas asked her to speak to their students on "race, beauty, and body image in the modeling industry." She offered her own stories and described her own experiences in the business. She was honest and forthright about what she saw in the fashion world. "The careers are so short and the competition is so strong, models tend to get very insecure. . . . I do feel the obligation to tell [young girls who write to me] that 99 percent of the modeling industry is fantasy."

Tyra's forthrightness about her profession did not in any way diminish her popularity as a guest speaker. She continued to accept speaking engagements at a variety of schools. Nor did her career suffer. She was busy and fulfilled. Her life had acquired a certain rhythm, a pattern that defined her life through her chosen activities: a fashion show here, a magazine shoot there, busy, but giving back to the community. She was working at her career, but keeping an eye toward progress—for kids, women, African Americans, and people like herself.

What more could Tyra Banks conquer? She found out in the fall of 1995 when another career breakthrough presented itself. *Sports Illustrated* chose her, along with another model, Valerie Mazza, to grace the cover of the upcoming *Sports Illustrated Swimsuit Issue*. Tyra Banks was about to become even more bankable.

7

TYRA BREAKS THE BARRIERS

MORE THAN 30 years ago, *Sports Illustrated*, the wildly popular male-oriented magazine, caught on to the idea that presenting models in skimpy outfits was sure to reap a monetary bonanza. Its annual *Swimsuit Issue*, which once was only an insert in the magazine, now stands by itself and has grown in popularity by leaps and bounds. *Sports Illustrated* claims that the *Swimsuit Issue* reaches 55 million readers. (About 24 million read the regular issues.)

Through its advertising, the *Swimsuit Issue* exerts a powerful influence on the modeling and swimwear industries. It has been said that this issue can make the career of a swimwear designer and propel a model into a superstar. Cheryl Tiegs appeared in 10 issues, and Christie Brinkley made the covers for three consecutive years. Tyra was quite aware of the impact that appearing on this magazine cover could have on her career and also that all previous covers had been modeled only by white women. Although she shared the 1996 honors with another model, appearing at all was an incredible triumph for Tyra, the first African American to appear on the *Swimsuit Issue* cover.

The theme of the issue in which Tyra was to appear was "South African Adventure," and she and Valerie Mazza visited that country for photo shoots. There, clad in skimpy cheetah-skin-print swimsuits,

Throughout her career, Tyra has broken barriers that have challenged so many African-American models. Her solo appearance on the cover of the 1997 Sports Illustrated Swimsuit Issue *was a first for a black woman. Here she celebrates her triumph with Elaine Farley, senior editor of the issue.*

she and Valerie posed together on a sunny beach.

There is no question that having one's image in the *Sports Illustrated Swimsuit Issue* can be a powerful springboard to success. Of her first cover, Tyra said, "The day it came out, I got on a plane, and everybody on the plane knew who I was. It was an overnight change." There is another instant change as well. Being featured on the cover of the *Swimsuit Issue* can vastly increase a model's fee.

Getting on prestigious covers does indeed bring changes and money. But a glossy cover does not reveal the hard work that went into creating it. To prepare for the photo shoot, Tyra had to get up at three in the morning and begin doing her makeup and hair about four. Then came the shoot itself, which lasted until about eight. She and the crew then rested until about four in the afternoon, when it was time to resume shooting until sundown. She admits the work schedule was grueling, but as she said, "You have to go with the flow."

Tyra is noted for her professionalism. She is punctual and prepared when she arrives for work. Many times at shows she does her own makeup. She began doing it early in her career when she got tired of having to stand in line waiting for the best makeup artist. She has been known to tote some 30 lipsticks and eye shadows, which she can apply once she finds out what the look is for the show.

She also insists on getting eight hours of sleep every night, which is not always possible. But she does not "hang out," and she is not into partying. She has said, "I treat this like a 9-to-5 job because modeling is my business."

Tyra is also a firm believer in regular exercise. She likes to work out early in the day when it is quiet and no one is around. She relishes the idea of the sun, the grass, and the solitude of her own thoughts. In Los Angeles she loves to run on the

beach, sometimes clocking three miles in one stretch. Indoors, she runs up and down the stairs. It has all paid off. As she said to one interviewer, "You should see me sprint through an airport with all my stuff."

Tyra scored another victory in 1996 when *Gentlemen's Quarterly* (GQ) presented her on its cover. Not only was Tyra the first woman ever to

Tyra and four other models appear at a press conference held by Sports Illustrated *to publicize its* Swimsuit Issue. *From left to right are Stacey Williams, Georgina Robertson, Rebecca Romijn, and, next to Tyra, Valerie Mazza, who shared the 1996 cover with Tyra.*

appear on the front of the magazine, she was the first African American. It was noted that *GQ* had gotten the edge on *Sports Illustrated* because it presented Tyra solo. Although Tyra was certainly delighted at her good fortune, she kept her accomplishment in perspective. "It's nice to be part of history and to be breaking barriers," she commented. "[But] it'll be nice one day to have no more 'firsts.' Just 50ths and 60ths and 70ths."

In spite of Tyra's several "firsts" as an African-American model, she is not immune to displays of racism and has experienced acts of prejudice and discrimination in her everyday life. Once in New York City, she and a friend stopped at a newsstand to buy a magazine whose cover displayed Tyra's image. When Tyra picked up the issue, the proprietor ordered her and her friend out of the store. Tyra's friend pointed out that it was Tyra on the cover, and the man responded with "I don't care. You all look alike." This was the kind of incident Tyra would learn to ignore as she pursued her profession.

Appearing on the magazine covers did wonders for Tyra's career. She was flooded with offers for big-name commercial work, including two advertising spots aired during the 1996 Super Bowl game. Ad time for such spots costs millions per minute.

One Super Bowl ad, a 30-second commercial for Pepsi, featured Tyra and two other models, Cindy Crawford and Bridget Hall, cooing over a newborn baby. Each model held a Pepsi in her hand.

The Nike ad ran a full minute, a long time for a commercial spot. The ad featured Tyra and a wooden puppet called Li'l Penny (whose voice was that of comic Chris Rock). In the spot shown at the Super Bowl, the puppet hosts a party and is joined by his idol Tyra Banks and celebrities who include Stevie Wonder and basketball player Gheorghe Muresan.

Viewers liked the catchy refrain from the commercial, and it often followed Tyra when she made appearances. "Making those spots is really fun," she explained, "[but] I can't walk down the street without someone calling out 'Stop the car, that's Tyra Banks, fool!'"

While Tyra was stopping traffic with this ad, she signed with another major client, McDonald's. The advertisement, called Gone Fishin', was created to promote the fast-food chain's fish products. Tyra appeared as a mermaid. Tyra's next assignment was appearing in a "milk mustache" ad for the National Milk Processor Promotion Board. Sporting the milk mustache, and posing in a white tank top and jeans, Tyra promoted milk drinking with such copy as "Girls, here's today's beauty tip. Think about you and your 10 best friends. Chances are 9 of you aren't getting enough calcium. So what? So milk. 3 glasses of milk a day give you the calcium your growing bones need. Tomorrow—what to do when you're taller than your date."

One of the most significant firsts in Tyra's life came when *Sports Illustrated* offered her another *Swimsuit Issue* cover for 1997. This time, she would appear solo. Emblazoned across the cover was the issue's feature for the year—"Nothing but Bikinis." Next to the headline stood Tyra, a gorgeous wind-blown figure in a tiny red-and-white polka-dot bikini. Inside the magazine, 16 pages of photos and text were devoted to Tyra. The coverage was more than twice as many pages as other models had received in past issues. The two *Sports Illustrated* and the *GQ* covers displayed Tyra to a male audience that had not previously paid attention to the women's magazines. It was a tremendous boost to her exposure as a model.

Further acclaim followed when Tyra signed an

Her face half covered by her long hair, Tyra models a wild print outfit in a Victoria's Secret fashion show. On the runway, Tyra shows off fashions in her own unique style, which has been described as a "sassy" walk and a "come-hither" expression.

exclusive contract with Victoria's Secret, pledging print, television, and fashion-show advertising. Star watchers hailed her sassy style as she strolled down the company's runways. Her incredible popularity led Victoria's Secret to put her on the cover of its catalog.

In 1997 Tyra undertook a somewhat different mission for Victoria's Secret. She agreed to a shoot for the unveiling of the company's three-million-dollar bra, which had been created by jeweler Harry Winston. Photographers and video crews, as well as eager fans, gathered on New York's Fifth Avenue to see her model the bejeweled piece of underwear.

The rumor floated that to protect Tyra and the bra's scores of diamonds an armored car would be used. As the press maneuvered for the best spots for photos, a huge armored car drew up. After a few moments of tension, Tyra emerged, dressed all in black. She posed for the press and then began to remove her clothes. The crowd gasped as she revealed the most expensive bra ever made. After posing with the bra, Tyra stayed for a question-and-answer period with the press. The big question was whether she would get to keep the diamond-studded piece of underwear. "I wish," Tyra replied.

Tyra also caused a stir when she modeled an ad for Swatch "skin" watches, billed as the thinnest timepieces in the world. For this spot, Tyra modeled nude, costumed only in the watch, although she did cross her arms over her chest. The ad campaign, called "Am I Naked? Or Am I Not?", was to commemorate the opening of a New York City Swatch store. Swatch's chief executive officer, Nicolas Hayek, expressed what many designers, advertisers, and fans would readily agree with: "[Tyra] is full of life, on the cutting edge of fashion, and always a little provocative."

Part of Tyra's contract with Swatch required her

to make public appearances throughout the United States, Europe, and Asia to promote the watch. During one appearance at a Swatch store, fans who were lined up to catch a glimpse of Tyra were rewarded with autographs. She happily signed her name on copies of the ad that featured the Swatch blurb and took time to talk to tourists from abroad. A day of ordinary sightseeing had offered those tourists an opportunity to meet one of the world's most famous supermodels.

Tyra has been asked whether she is bothered when people ask for autographs. She understands that fans want some part of her, and she does not mind if they ask—except when she is in a restaurant. She considers it rude to be interrupted when she is dining. Tyra is also accommodating when fans ask if they can take their picture with her.

When Tyra posed for the 1998 *Sports Illustrated Swimsuit Calendar*, it became an instant bestseller. It was so successful that Tyra flew to Hawaii to shoot another calendar for 1999.

Tyra has not always taken all the opportunities that come her way. For example, some companies produce dolls of famous models. Although Tyra has received such offers, she refuses to promote her image through these spin-offs. She admits that she has exposed quite a bit of herself on calendars and magazine covers. There is, however, a limit to how she will allow her name to be used, and dolls she characterizes as "cheesy." That is a line, she declares, she will not cross.

Tyra had also done some music videos. When the singer Lionel Richie needed a star for his video *Don't Want to Lose*, he asked Tyra to play the role of his girlfriend. In the video Tyra is a rising star who rushes in and out of limousines, avoids harassing photographers, and is surrounded by bodyguards. Richie was delighted with her performance, and Tyra and her mother agreed that she looked her

most beautiful in the video. Three other videos followed as she appeared in Michael Jackson's *Black and White*, George Michaels's *Too Funky*, and Tina Turner's *Love Thing*.

With all of the publicity and promotions associated with Tyra's innumerable projects, she has enlisted a loyal cadre of fans. In spite of her stardom, she is still awed by the attention she receives and has described her feelings:

> I'm still amazed when I see a huge crowd of fans show up for an autograph signing, or when photographers jump in my face, clicking away, both at my public appearances and in my private life. Sometimes I turn around to see who they are waiting for, and when I realize that it's me I have to laugh and shake my head.

Tyra enjoys a laugh with Swatch CEO Nicolas Hayek, who was delighted with her modeling for the company's Swatch skin watches. Hayek enthused that Tyra "is the embodiment of Swatch's winning characteristics."

Tyra takes a moment from her appearance at an after-school activity center to give an enthusiastic hug to a young fan. For her legions of loyal fans, Tyra is a role model of how determination and hard work can overcome both personal and professional challenges.

Tyra's fans can find out more about her using the computer to access the major Tyra phenomenon on the Internet. A one-time name search under "Tyra" could elicit more than 200,000 matches. Notes of every sort about Tyra can be found: articles, listings, photos, love poems, and descriptive comments. One fan even took the trouble to think up 16 anagrams for "Tyra Banks." Such an outpouring of interest could only mean that Tyra Banks is here to stay.

The young supermodel's numerous projects have brought her phenomenal success and millions of dollars. By carefully selecting her jobs and diversifying, she could look forward to creating many more possibilities for the future.

8

"YA' GOTTA LOVE THE FOOL IN YOU"

WITH SO MANY achievements behind her, Tyra could take a deep breath and ask herself what was important now for her personal and professional development. She expressed her ideas about one's personal life when she made an appearance on the television show *Good Morning America*. She advised teenagers, "Ya' gotta love the fool in you as well as the part that's got it goin' on."

She urged young people to understand that what they see in the mirror is important but that more important is how they feel about themselves. For Tyra, self-love is an invaluable part of life, and she believes that caring about oneself equals self-esteem. She is convinced that when people work to help others, they will create good feelings about themselves. Amid all her successes and fame, she has been determined to exemplify this philosophy.

Tyra has not wavered from the responsibility she feels to be honest with young women about beauty, the truth of the fashion world, and the importance of drawing strength from within themselves. Remembering her own often insecure feelings as a child and teen, she is determined to help other girls and young women feel comfortable with their bodies and minds.

With this objective in mind, Tyra wrote her

Tyra's philosophy is that you learn self-esteem by caring about yourself. This is the message she consistently urges young people to embrace.

beauty-and-life advice book, *Tyra's Beauty, Inside and Out*. Much of the book is also autobiographical. She has explained her reasons for writing the book:

> Some of you may look at me and think, "That girl never had an insecure day in her life." Well, I think my experiences will prove that you can't always judge a book by its cover (not even this one). I've struggled with chronic warts, poor body image, and one too many broken hearts on the road to supermodel status. And I know all about the pressure we're put under to be perfect. . . . Between the life lessons I've learned and practical tips I've added from my friends in the fashion biz, this book will show you how *to look and feel beautiful—inside and out*.

In her book, Tyra discusses an array of problems and questions about almost any subject that concerns young people: beauty, friends, sex, parents, health, work, facing challenges, overcoming adversity, building self-esteem—just name it. Using stories, anecdotes, letters from young people, and descriptions of her own life experiences, Tyra encourages young people to overcome obstacles and reach their goals.

Tyra has said that without the aid of her journals, she would probably not have been able to write her book. Since she was seven years old she has been jotting down experiences, interesting events, ideas, and comments about friends and family. Keeping a journal has been for her a form of relaxation, freeing her from tensions and stress. Tyra likes to thumb back through her journals to remind herself of how she reacted to an event or handled a situation.

Because Tyra is especially concerned about the misuse of drugs and alcohol as an answer to life's problems, she advises readers of alternative ways to feel good when they are down. In what she calls "five feel-good mood busters," Tyra details these alternatives:

To promote her book, Tyra's Beauty, Inside and Out, *Tyra appeared at scores of book signings. In a tribute to those who had helped make her success possible, she dedicated the book to "the women before me who paved the way," as well as to her mother and father for their love and support.*

- Get in touch with a close friend, one who you know will lift your spirits, and talk it out.

- Don't be afraid to spoil yourself. Indulge in a long, hot bubble bath or play some soothing music by candlelight.

- Get a funny video or watch a sitcom and laugh yourself into stitches.

- For many people prayer or meditation can be a wonderful mood lifter. For others time alone to think your own thoughts can help put troubles into perspective.

- Give of yourself in volunteer work. When you get a good feeling from helping others, it is hard to be self-destructive.

Tyra's book was published in the early spring of 1998, and by the end of the year had been named one of *School Library Journal*'s Best Books of 1998. Tyra introduced her book when she appeared at the Volunteerism Awards. It had its more formal debut at a Crown Books bookstore in Washington, D.C. *Tyra's Beauty* and its acceptance were the culmination of all the work she had done to promote a message dear to her heart.

What of her career, or perhaps what could be called her "second" career as an actor? Tyra thoroughly enjoyed her brief stint in films, and she wanted to further pursue filmmaking. Doing films gave her a chance to implement one of her newly affirmed goals, reawakened from her high-school days: film and television production.

Following her role in *The Fresh Prince of Bel-Air*, Tyra had appeared in three episodes of the Fox television series *New York Undercover*. Then when Disney studios found a starring vehicle for her, *Honey Thunder Dunk*, a television movie to be presented on *The Wonderful World of Disney*, she jumped at the chance. In her first film for television, she would not only

Wearing a WNBA New York Liberty shirt, Tyra takes a bow at a basketball game, a sport she learned to love as a child. She likes to play as well, reporting that she can pass, dribble, and steal but can't shoot.

be the star but the coproducer. The film needed an athletic type, and the other producers had developed the story with Tyra in mind. Described as a romantic comedy, the film is set in the world of basketball, and Tyra's role is that of a player in the Women's National Basketball Association (WNBA).

In the movie, Tyra's challenge is not to play basketball but to contend with a male ball player who cannot make it in men's basketball and joins the women's team. Disguised as a woman, he is the only "female" player who can dunk. He falls for Tyra's character, who thinks the guy is a gal, and that is where the fun begins. For Tyra, the film is especially enjoyable because she is an avid basketball fan as well as a spokesperson for the WNBA.

Another film Tyra became involved in was an independent production, which began shooting in the summer of 1998. The movie is called *Love Stinks*, a title in keeping with its billing as an "unromantic comedy." Tyra's costars include Bridgette Wilson, Jason Bateman, Bill Bellamy, and French Stewart from the television show *Third Rock from the Sun*. "We've got a great cast," commented one of the producers, "and Tyra and Bridgette have been really funny together in rehearsal."

When the cable channel Showtime unveiled its upcoming slate for 1999, it announced a starring role for Tyra in the film *The Apartment Complex*. Her costars in this production are Chad Lowe, Amanda Plummer, and Patrick Warburton. The film concerns a psychology student who manages a weird building: one of the apartments seems to be missing.

At one point a rumor surfaced that Tyra had taken up a singing career. It was all a mistake that came about when the English magazine *Sky* misinterpreted a headline in an American paper. Tyra had just signed for a cosmetics' deal for a hefty sum of money, and the headline declared "Fresh Prince Girl Tyra Gets Record Deal." *Sky*, however, completely changed the headline around: "Tyra Signs Record Deal with Prince." Tyra vehemently denied the rumor. "I only ever sing in the shower," she explained, "and then it's usually just a bit of Alanis Morissette, because I like the screaming." At one time, however, Tyra did admit she would like to

play a singer in a movie but said she would defi-
nitely leave the singing part to others.

With the hectic schedule of fashion shows, modeling, special appearances, and television and filmmaking, how does Tyra deal with her personal life?
She has always been and still is very close to her
family, especially her mother, who has been Tyra's
mentor throughout her career and her manager for
the past seven years. Tyra refers to Carolyn as
"supermom" and says it is "sometimes hard to draw
the line between mom and manager."

Carolyn is an energetic woman who cannot
seem to sit still for a minute. She often carries a box
of tools around with her in case something breaks
down. She always lends a helping hand to others
and does not seem to know when to say no. Tyra
attributes much of her own energy to her mother's
example. And Tyra's abhorrence of drugs comes
from her mother's values. Carolyn did not lecture
Tyra about the horrors of addiction. She simply
talked to her daughter about friends who had ruined
their lives with drugs. For Tyra, the love, guidance,
and confidence instilled in her by her mother and
all the members of her family has been a major influence in shaping her self-esteem.

Although a celebrity who could attract all the
guys she wanted, Tyra has not had many serious
romances in her life. She did date John Singleton for
a time when they making *Higher Learning* together.
Singleton, who admired her beauty and talent, once
said that "She brought out the silly side in me that
no one else is allowed to see." The romance did not
last, however.

Tyra also had a serious romance with singer, song-
writer, and pop-music icon Seal. Born Sealhenry
Samuel, he was at 33 more than 10 years older than
Tyra when they dated. But his 6′4″ frame did match
her height. Of their relationship at the time, Seal

Tyra and director John Singleton, her former boyfriend, appear at a screening of their film Higher Learning. Some felt that Tyra got the role because she and Singleton were dating at the time. Tyra shrugged off their suspicions and kept on working.

commented, "We're happy together. We're taking it slowly." Tyra declared that she loved him very much and described him as "the most special man I know." This relationship, too, broke up, and in 1997 Tyra declared that she no longer wanted to date celebrities and those she characterized as "model groupies." She just wanted to be with a normal guy.

At this point in her life, Tyra has definite ideas about married or otherwise attached men. They are off limits for her. She says that she has been cheated on, and it devastated her. Any of her friends who try to appropriate a boyfriend are off her list for good. In her book, she strongly advises young women to follow this example and save themselves from such wrenching experiences.

Although Tyra does not believe in identifying herself through men, she does have definite ideas of the kind of man she would like. He had better have a sense of humor, along with old-fashioned virtues. By those, Tyra means being prompt, pulling out her chair, opening doors for her. He should also have no problem about splitting a check. She has not yet found this "perfect" man.

Tyra did not move from her parents' home until she was 21. After making the film *Higher Learning*, she bought her own house in Los Angeles. A five-bedroom, Mediterranean-style home with a patio and Spanish fountain, it was a peaceful retreat from her heavy schedule of traveling. She did later admit, however, that buying the house might have been a mistake because she was often lonely there.

Recently Tyra purchased another home outside Orlando, Florida. She planned her new home to be bright, like the Florida sun, and whimsical and fun. It is a place where she can relax and be herself. Part of the reason for choosing Orlando is that she does a lot of work in Florida. Another is so that she can visit Disney World and other theme parks. Going to amusement parks is one of Tyra's ways of having fun.

Tyra is an avid runner, who runs not only for exercise but also just for the pleasure of it. Running is Tyra's second love, however. Her first is dancing. As a child she took ballet and jazz-dancing lessons, and she continues to indulge her favorite pastime, by combining workouts with dance. She especially likes dancing to drums and she loses herself in their rhythms, dancing and swaying to the beat.

Listening to music is also one of Tyra's pleasures. She enjoys Alanis Morrisette, Snoop, Jewel, and The Cranberries. And even though she is a film star, she still loves going to the movies. In fact, she likes to go alone. Tyra is also a basketball fan, a sport she learned to like from her father, who took her to Los Angeles Lakers games. When she can, she attends Lakers games and has a courtside seat. She is particularly pleased about the establishment of the Women's National Basketball Association and is an avid spectator at their games, too.

Tyra really enjoys shopping. She loves to browse through thrift shops, a holdover from her high-school days. She is a jeans addict and looks for the vintage kind. New ones are too stiff, and as she says "don't hug [her] in the right places." Since she is fussy, she has a lot of patience and does not mind examining endless racks of clothes. Her closet bulges with outfits of every imaginable style and color.

As Tyra looks back on her achievements, all attained by the age of 25, she can be proud of her life and the way she has lived it. She can see how her perseverance, professionalism, and determination turned opportunity into a dazzling career. She can see that the values she learned growing up translated into working for the good of others. In the future, Tyra plans to continue to choose her material carefully and bend her efforts to promote opportunities and respect for all African Americans.

Looking forward, Tyra also sees careers in films, television, and production that she can pursue should modeling no longer be an option. Or perhaps she will break new ground for mature models. When she diversified her career, she discovered how flexible she could be. "No matter how famous you are," she once said, "so much of modeling is waiting for the next job. I want to be the one who does the hiring, not the one who's waiting to be hired."

Tyra Banks knows herself well. She is aware that the real world does not revolve around supermodel Tyra. But she knows the real world has gained because she has lent it a bit of herself.

CHRONOLOGY

———— ❧ ————

1973   Tyra Lynn Banks is born on December 4th in Inglewood, California.

1978   Enters International Children's School in Los Angeles.

1979   Parents Don and Carolyn London Banks divorce.

1983   Mother marries Clifford Johnson Jr.

1985   Shoots up to 5′9″, growing three inches and losing 20 pounds in three months.

1987   Enters Immaculate Heart High School.

1989   Signs with first modeling agency, L.A. Models, Los Angeles.

1991   Graduates from Immaculate Heart High School; receives offer from a French modeling agency to work in Paris for one year; shoots first magazine cover, *20 Ans*, in Paris; books for unprecedented 25 fashion shows in one week during her first season; works with designers Chanel, Christian Dior, and Yves St. Laurent.

1992   Returns to Los Angeles; establishes Tyra Banks Scholarship for African-American girls at Immaculate Heart; creates her own corporation, Ty Girl Corporation.

1993   Plays role of Jackie Ames on TV show *The Fresh Prince of Bel-Air*; signs exclusive modeling contract with Cover Girl cosmetics, only third African-American female model to do so.

1994   Stars in movie *Higher Learning*.

1995   Becomes spokesperson for Center for Children + Families in New York City; begins series of lectures on race, beauty, and body image in the modeling industry at various schools and universities around the country.

1996   Shares *Sports Illustrated Swimsuit Issue* cover with model Valeria Mazza; first woman and first black model to be featured on GQ magazine cover; appears in television commercials: Nike's "Li'l Penny," McDonald's "Gone Fishin'"; does "milk mustache" print ad for National Milk Processor Promotion Board.

1997   First African-American model to be featured solo on the *Sports Illustrated Swimsuit Issue* cover; signs exclusive contract as model and spokesperson for Swatch watches; signs exclusive contract with Victoria's Secret and becomes first black model on its catalog cover; establishes and organizes Kidshare event for needy children; 1998 *Sports Illustrated Swimsuit Calendar* featuring Tyra Banks released; guest stars on three episodes of Fox TV's *New York Undercover*; receives the Friendship Award from the Starlight Children's Foundation for her work with children; renames Ty Girl Corporation to Bankable, Inc.

1998   Publishes *Tyra's Beauty, Inside and Out*, which is listed in *School Library Journal*'s Best Books of 1998; speaks at Volunteerism Awards for Cover Girl cosmetics and *Seventeen* magazine; shoots 1999 *Sports Illustrated Swimsuit Calendar* featuring Tyra Banks; begins production of films *Love Stinks* and *The Apartment Complex*; coproduces and stars in Disney television movie *Honey Thunder Dunk*; begins developing official Tyra Banks website, www.tyratyratyra.com.

1999   Hosts the 13th annual Soul Train Music Awards; featured on the cover of the 4th Anniversary Special, April 1999, issue of *P.O.V. (Point of View)*, along with an article on confidence published in the same issue; featured on the cover of *Celebrity Sleuth*, vol. 12, no. 3.

FURTHER READING

———— ❧ ————

Banks, Tyra, and Vanessa Thomas Bush. *Tyra's Beauty, Inside and Out.* New York: Harper-Collins Publishers, 1998.

Fine, Sam, and Julia Chance. *Fine Beauty: Beauty Basics and Beyond for African American Women.* New York: Riverhead Books, 1998.

Gross, Michael. *Model: the Ugly Business of Beautiful Women.* New York: William Morrow and Co., 1995.

Hamilton, Bill. *The Art of the Walk.* New York: HarperCollins, 1998.

Morris, Sandra. *Catwalk: Inside the World of the Supermodels.* New York: Universe Publishers, 1996.

Rubinstein, Donna, and Jennifer Kingson Bloom. *The Modeling Life.* New York: Putnam Publishing Group, 1998.

White, Constance. *Style Noir: The First How-to Guide to Fashion Written with Black Women in Mind.* New York: Berkeley Publishing Group, 1998.

INTERNET RESOURCES

http://www.cnnsi.com or www.sportsillustrated.com
  [CNN/Sports Illustrated site, includes information on *Sports Illustrated* magazine and on Super Bowl advertising]

http://www.covergirl.com
  [official Cover Girl site, includes model biographies and photos]

http://www.ellemag.com
  [portfolios of seven supermodels, including Tyra Banks]

http://www.fashionangel.com
  [broad directory on fashion, beauty, modeling; includes a link to Femme Fatale Productions, which focuses "on promoting a true and accurate image of the diverse beauty and unique style of the African-American woman"]

http://www.phys.com
  [*Glamour, Mademoiselle, Vogue, Self, Allure, Condé Nast Sports for Women* magazines online]

http://www.supermodel.com
  [models, modeling, fashion; search /newswire for "Tyra"]

http://www.swatch.com
  [official Swatch site, includes small Tyra Banks section]

http://www.swoon.com
  [*Glamour, Mademoiselle, Details, GQ* magazines online]

http://www.tyratyratyra.com
  [official Tyra Banks website]

INDEX

PICTURE CREDITS

PAM LEVIN lived in Milan, Italy, for three years. She now lives in Washington, D.C., with her young daughter, Olivia. Her previous book for Chelsea House was on the life and work of Susan B. Anthony.

NATHAN IRVIN HUGGINS, one of America's leading scholars in the field of black studies, helped select the titles for the BLACK AMERICANS OF ACHIEVEMENT series, for which he also served as senior consulting editor. He was the W. E. B. DuBois Professor of History and Afro-American Studies at Harvard University and the director of the W. E. B. DuBois Institute for Afro-American Research at Harvard. He received his doctorate from Harvard in 1962 and returned there as professor in 1980 after teaching at Columbia University, the University of Massachusetts, Lake Forest College, and the California State University, Long Beach. He was the author of four books and dozens of articles, including *Black Odyssey: The Afro-American Ordeal in Slavery*, *The Harlem Renaissance*, and *Slave and Citizen: The Life of Frederick Douglass*, and was associated with the Children's Television Workshop, National Public Radio, the Boston Athenaeum, the Museum of Afro-American History, the Howard Thurman Educational Trust, and Upward Bound. Professor Huggins died in 1989, at the age of 62, in Cambridge, Massachusetts.